CHICKEN

Sunset Creative Cooking Library

By the Editors of Sunset Books

SUNSET BOOKS
President & Publisher: Susan J. Maruyama
Director, Finance & Business Affairs: Gary Loebner
**Director, Manufacturing
& Sales Service:** Lorinda Reichert

SUNSET PUBLISHING CORPORATION
Chairman: Robert L. Miller
President/Chief Executive Officer: Robin Wolaner
Chief Financial Officer: James E. Mitchell
Circulation Director: Robert I. Gursha
Editor, Sunset Magazine: William R. Marken

All the recipes in this book were developed and tested
in the Sunset test kitchens. For information about any
Sunset Book please call 1-800-634-3095.

The nutritional data provided for each recipe is for
a single serving, based on the number of servings and
the amount of each ingredient. If a range is given for the
number of servings and/or the amount of an ingredient,
the analysis is based on the average of the figures given.
The nutritional analysis does not include optional ingredients or those for which no specific amount is stated.
If an ingredient is listed with a substitution, the data was
calculated using the first choice.

Nutritional analysis of recipes: Hill Nutrition
Associates, Inc. of Florida.

Sunset Creative Cooking Library
was produced by St. Remy Press

Publisher: Kenneth Winchester
President: Pierre Léveillé
Managing Editor: Carolyn Jackson
Senior Editors: Elizabeth Cameron, Dianne Thomas
Managing Art Director: Diane Denoncourt
Administrator: Natalie Watanabe
Production Manager: Michelle Turbide
System Coordinator: Jean-Luc Roy
Proofreader: Jennifer Meltzer
Indexer: Christine Jacobs

COVER: *Chicken & Fruit Kebabs (page 63)*

PHOTOGRAPHY
*Victor Budnik: 26, 42, 62; Robert Chartier: 17, 24, 41,
51, 55, 61; Glenn Christiansen: 20; Peter Christiansen:
14, 22, 28; Kevin Sanchez: 18, 32, 38, 58; Darrow M.
Watt: 4, 5, 36; Tom Wyatt: 30, 46, 48, 52, 56; Nikolay
Zurek: 12, 44.*

PHOTO STYLING
*JoAnn Masaoka Van Atta: 12, 44, 26, 46;
Susan Massey-Weil: 18, 30, 32, 38, 48, 52, 56, 58;
Lynne B. Morrall: 42, 62.*

ISBN 0-376-00900-4
Library of Congress Catalog Card Number 94-67314
Printed in the United States.

✪ printed on recycled paper.

Table of Contents

How to Truss & Roast Chicken

What is trussing? It's simply securing the wings and legs of poultry to its body with string. You can truss or not, depending on your personal preference. Some experienced cooks always roast birds without trussing. But trussing has several advantages: it ensures moist, tender meat by preventing the skin from splitting at the joints, and it provides a compact, well-shaped bird that's easy to carve.

There are many ways to truss poultry, but we show you how to do it with a trussing needle. You can purchase this needle at gourmet cookware shops or in the housewares section of many department stores. The needle must be long enough to penetrate the bird's body and extend about an inch from both wings. For a chicken weighing 3 to 4 pounds, you'll need an 8-inch trussing needle.

Use only white cotton string; colored string will bleed onto the meat, and polyester string may shrink during baking, tearing the bird's skin.

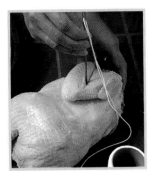

1. Insert trussing needle into flesh between wing joints; push needle through body cavity, exiting between wing joints on other side. Pull string through.

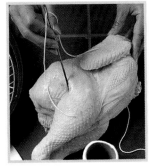

2. Insert needle at an angle between thigh and leg joint, and push toward body cavity. Tucking end under, fold tail skin over breast skin.

3. Exit needle through tail. Stitching in and out about 3 times, secure tail, closing cavity. Push needle through opposite thigh and leg joint.

How to Roast

Preheat the oven to 375°F. Rinse the chicken inside and out and pat dry with paper towels. If you wish, stuff the bird.

To estimate total cooking time, multiply the chicken's weight by 20 to 25 minutes per pound. Use the same roasting time whether the bird is stuffed or not.

Place the prepared bird, breast side up, on a rack in a shallow roasting pan. Generously smear its skin with softened butter, or follow your recipe instructions. For a large bird, insert a meat thermometer into the thickest part of the thigh, without touching bone.

During the last half of the roasting time, baste with pan juices every 15 minutes to keep the chicken moist. Check the thermometer toward the end of the estimated time; when it registers 185°, the bird is done. For a small chicken, jiggle the drumstick; if it moves freely, the bird is done.

Remove the cooked bird from the oven; let stand 15 minutes before carving.

4. Turn bird on its side. Cut string, leaving about 4 inches on each end. Pull string taut from both ends; tie securely and trim excess string.

5. Bring legs together and tie securely with another length of string; trim excess.

6. After roasting, snip long string once and pull out; cut and remove leg string. Beautifully compact, golden chicken is star attraction at any meal.

Cutting up a Whole Bird

When you plan to bake chicken pieces—or cook them by any of the other methods detailed in this book—you'll save money if you buy a whole bird and cut it up in your own kitchen.

Using the step-by-step instructions illustrated at right, you can learn to cut up a chicken quickly. When you cut up a bird yourself, don't throw anything away. The giblets can flavor gravy and the bones make a flavorful broth (page 9).

Fresh poultry is perishable and should be cooked within two days. If you're not planning to cook the giblets with the bird, freeze the heart and gizzard in one container and the liver in another.

Nutritional Values of Poultry

One of the reasons poultry is so popular on healthy menus today is because it's easy to control the amount of fat you're eating; most of it lies just beneath the skin, where it can be removed when the skin is pulled off. What remains is high-quality protein in a relatively lean package.

As indicated in the chart below, breast (light) meat is lower in fat than leg (dark) meat. The amount of cholesterol in poultry is comparable to that in lean beef.

The chart is based on a portion size of 3 ounces of cooked poultry. Although some pieces, such as half a boneless chicken breast, may run larger, they can still be considered an acceptable portion.

Portion: 3 ounces cooked	Calories	Protein (g)	Total Fat (g)	Saturated Fat (g)	Cholesterol (mg)
Breast meat and skin, roasted	168	25	7	2	71
Breast meat only, roasted	140	26	3	1	72
Thigh meat and skin, roasted	210	21	13	4	79
Thigh meat only, roasted	178	22	9	3	81
Drumstick meat and skin, roasted	184	23	9	3	77
Drumstick meat only, roasted	146	24	5	1	79

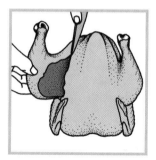

1. To remove leg and thigh, grasp leg and pull away from body. Cut through skin, exposing joint. Bend thigh back from body; cut close to body through hip joint. Repeat with other leg.

2. To separate leg from thigh, cut through skin between joints. Then bend leg back from thigh to expose joint; cut through joint; then cut through bottom portion of skin.

3. To remove wing, pull away from body. Cut through skin to expose shoulder joint; cut through joint. To remove wing tip, cut through joint. Repeat with wing on other side.

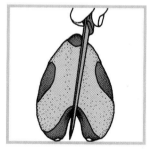

4. To separate chicken back from the breast, cut along each side of the backbone between the rib joints.

5. Bend the back piece in half at joint. (This is a natural break.) Cut, as shown above, to separate.

6. To split breast, place breast skin side up; cut through skin and meat along one side of breastbone. (To bone breast, see page 8.)

How to Bone a Chicken Breast

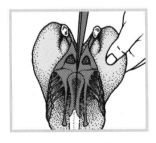

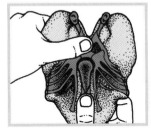

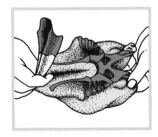

1. Lay breast skin side down; run a sharp knife down center to cut thin membrane and expose keel bone (dark spoon-shaped bone) and thick white cartilage.

2. Placing one thumb on tip of keel bone and other at rib cage base, grasp breast firmly. Bend breast back with both hands until keel bone breaks through.

3. Carefully run finger under edge of keel bone and thick cartilage, then pull out and discard.

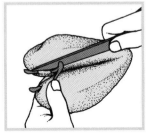

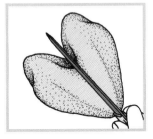

4. Insert knife under long first rib. Resting knife against bones, scrape meat away from bones. Cut rib away, and sever and remove shoulder joint. Repeat with other side of breast.

5. With fingers, locate wishbone. Cutting close to bone, remove wishbone.

6. Lay breast meat flat on a cutting board and cut breast in half; remove white tendon from bottom side of each half. Pull off skin, if suggested in recipe.

CHICKEN

Chicken Know-how

Star attraction of a traditional Sunday dinner, a festive holiday table, or even an ordinary week-day meal, chicken carries the day for all-around reliable goodness.

For one thing, few foods offer such succulence and natural richness of flavor, as does chicken. It also ranks among the best dinner bargains and is easy to prepare. Using the tips below, you can accent your cooking with home-made chicken broth, and cook any chicken—whole or in parts—to absolute perfection every time.

Making home-cooked chicken broth. One obvious economy of cutting up a chicken at home is that nothing need go to waste. For our richly flavored broth, save wing tips, backs, necks, and even the breastbones and skins from boned chicken breasts. Collect them in a gallon-size freezer bag and store them in the freezer until you have 3 to 4 pounds.

Home-cooked chicken broth is easy enough to make, and makes a noticeable improvement over canned broth. Place 3 to 4 pounds chicken bones in an 8-quart pan. Add 1 large onion, quartered; 1 carrot, cut into chunks; 1 stalk celery; 2 sprigs parsley; 1 bay leaf; ¼ teaspoon thyme leaves; and 2 quarts cold water.

Bring ingredients to a boil over high heat; then reduce heat and simmer, partially covered, for 2 to 3 hours. Strain; discard vegetables and bones. Season to taste with salt and pepper. Skim off the fat.

If made ahead, cool, cover, and refrigerate for up to 3 days; freeze for longer storage. Makes about 1 quart of broth.

Testing for doneness. The cooking method and type of recipe you use determine how you'll check a bird for doneness.

• When testing chicken pieces that have been sautéed, fried, baked, or braised, cut a gash in the thickest part of one piece—the meat should not be pink and the juices should run clear yellow when the meat is done.

• If you're cooking both breasts and thighs at the same time, make sure it is the thighs you test for doneness, as they take longer to cook.

• There are several ways to test roasted whole birds. Jiggle a leg—it should move freely. Or prick the meat near the thigh joint with a fork; when the juices run clear yellow, the bird is done. The most accurate way to test roasted chicken, however, is to use a meat thermometer. Insert it into the thickest portion of the thigh, taking care that the thermometer does not touch a bone, and roast until the thermometer registers 185°.

The Basics of Barbecuing

Barbecuing is one culinary art that even a novice backyard chef can master with ease. Of course, it's crucial that you use your equipment properly and learn a few basic skills.

Types of barbecues. Barbecues are available in three main types (charcoal-fired, gas, and electric) and dozens of styles. Your choice will depend on where you'll use your barbecue, the number of people you'll usually be serving, and the kinds of food you're most likely to barbecue.

Charcoal-fired barbecues. The most popular models are open braziers, covered kettles of various sizes, and boxes with hinged lids.

• Open braziers vary from tabletop portables and hibachis to large models for quantity cooking. Many feature a cooking grill that can be raised or lowered to adjust the distance between the charcoal and food, thus controlling the heat.

• Covered kettles are available in various sizes. Dampers on the lid and under the firebox allow you to adjust the flow of air and control the heat. A covered kettle is ideal for cooking large cuts of meat, since it provides the same even heat an oven does.

• Kettle barbecues may also be used, either

Two Ways to Barbecue

By direct heat. Open the bottom dampers if your barbecue has them. Spread briquets on the fire grate in a solid layer that's 1 to 2 inches bigger all around than the grill area required for the food. Then mound the charcoal and ignite it. When the coals have reached the fire temperature specified in the recipe, spread them out into a single layer again. Set the grill at the recommended height above coals. (Fire temperature is described in Barbecuing Tips on page 11).

By indirect heat. Open or remove the lid from a covered barbecue, then open the bottom dampers. Pile approximately 50 long-burning briquets on the fire grate and ignite them. Let the briquets burn until hot; this usually takes about 30 minutes. Using long-handled tongs, bank about half the briquets on each side of the fire grate; then place a metal drip pan in the center. Set the cooking grill 4 to 6 inches above the pan. Set the food on the grill directly above the drip pan. If you're grilling meat, place it fat side up.

uncovered or covered, for grilling over direct heat. Leaving the lid off does make it easier to watch, but many manufacturers recommend covering the grill to speed up cooking, conserve fuel, and control flare-ups.

• Barbecue boxes with hinged lids are similar to covered kettles, and can be used covered for cooking by indirect heat, or open or closed for grilling over direct heat. They have adjustable dampers for heat control; many also have adjustable charcoal pans that can be raised and lowered. Spit-roasting attachments are sometimes available.

Gas & electric barbecues. Outdoor units fueled by bottled gas usually roll on wheels; natural gas units are mounted on a fixed pedestal and must be connected to a permanent gas line. Electric units are portable; they can be plugged into the nearest outlet. All gas units and some electric models employ a special briquet-shaped material, such as lava rock, above the burner. When meat juices drip on these hot "briquets," smoke rises to penetrate and flavor the food.

Gas and electric barbecues save you the work of building the fire and cleaning up ashes. And most units require only a brief preheating, so you can start cooking in a matter of minutes. As a rule, food grilled on these barbecues cooks in about the same time as on charcoal-fired models.

Barbecuing Tips

• All the recipes in this book were tested on a charcoal-fueled barbecue, using 2-inch pressed briquets.

• Most of the recipes were tested with the cooking grill 4 to 6 inches above the coals. If your grill is closer, the cooking time will be shorter.

• Use the fire temperature recommended in the recipe. *Hot* coals are barely covered with gray ash; you can hold your hand near the grill for only 2 to 3 seconds. *Medium* coals glow through a layer of gray ash; you can hold your hand near the grill for only 4 to 5 seconds. *Low* describes coals covered with a thick layer of gray ash. You can hold your hand near the grill for 6 to 7 seconds.

• Always use potholders or mitts and long-handled cooking tools.

• Use a water-filled spray bottle to extinguish flare-ups.

• Turn food with tongs or a spatula—a fork pierces, allowing juices to escape.

• Salt food *after* cooking (salt draws out juices).

• To prevent steaks and chops from curling, slash edge fat at 2- to 3-inch intervals; cut *just to meat.*

SOUP & SALAD FARE

Chicken & Capellini Soup

Tender strands of capellini swirl through this appetizing chicken-vegetable soup. Enjoy it with a loaf of crusty Italian bread, a selection of cheeses, and sliced ripe pears or crisp apples.

⌒

PER SERVING: *305 calories, 38 g protein, 17 g carbohydrates, 9 g total fat, 101 mg cholesterol, 926 mg sodium*

PREPARATION TIME : *15 min.*
COOKING TIME: *30 min.*

2 whole chicken breasts
   (1 lb. each), skinned, boned
2 Tbsp. butter or margarine
¼ cup finely chopped shallots
1 clove pressed garlic
¼ tsp. salt
¼ tsp. dry thyme
⅛ tsp. ground white pepper
1 can (14½ oz.) chicken
   broth
1½ cups water
½ cup dry white wine
1 carrot, thinly sliced
2 oz. dry capellini
2 cups shredded Swiss
   chard leaves
1 tomato, seeded, chopped
Grated Parmesan cheese

Cut chicken into ½-inch cubes. Melt butter in a 3½- to 4-quart pan over medium heat. Add shallots and cook, stirring often, until soft but not browned (2 to 3 minutes). Stir in garlic, salt, thyme, white pepper, and chicken. Cook, stirring often, until chicken looks opaque (about 3 minutes). Add broth, water, wine, and carrot. Bring to a boil over high heat; reduce heat, cover, and boil gently until carrot is tender to bite (about 15 minutes).

Break capellini strands in half; add capellini to soup and return to a boil. Cook, uncovered, stirring often, until pasta is al dente (4 to 5 minutes). Add chard and tomato; cover, remove from heat, and let stand just until tomato is heated through (about 2 minutes). Ladle into bowls; offer cheese as garnish.

Makes 4 servings

Gingered Broth
with Persimmon & Chicken

For dramatic presentation, arrange whole snow peas, thin wedges of persimmon, and thinly sliced green onion in wide bowls. As your guests watch, ladle seasoned broth with chicken over the fruit and vegetables.

⌒

PER SERVING: *180 calories, 13 g protein, 18 g carbohydrates, 2 g total fat, 22 mg cholesterol, 1188 mg sodium*

PREPARATION TIME: *30 min.*
COOKING TIME: *1 min.*

1/2 lb. boned, skinned chicken breasts, sliced paper-thin
1 Tbsp. soy sauce
1 tsp. Oriental sesame oil or toasted almond oil (optional)
1 1/2 qt. chicken broth
1 cup dry sherry
2 Tbsp. minced fresh ginger
1 star anise (or 1/2 tsp. anise seed and 3-inch-long cinnamon stick)
1 large (about 8 oz.) firm Fuyu persimmon, peeled, stemmed, cut in thin wedges
20 to 30 small (2 to 3 oz. total) snow peas, strings removed
1/3 cup sliced green onions

In a small bowl, mix chicken, soy sauce, and sesame oil. If made ahead, cover and chill up until next day.

In a 3- to 4-quart pan, combine chicken broth, dry sherry, fresh ginger, and star anise. Bring to a boil; cover and simmer for about 30 minutes. If desired, discard spices.

In each of 6 wide, shallow bowls (about 1 1/2-cup size), arrange equal portions of persimmon, peas, and green onions; bring bowls to the table.

Heat gingered broth to boiling on the range or on a portable burner at the table. Stir in chicken; simmer just until chicken is opaque, 30 seconds to 1 minute. If cooking broth on range, pour into a tureen and bring to the table. Carefully ladle broth into each bowl over fruit and vegetables.

Makes 6 servings

Chicken Barley Soup

Fresh oranges and crushed anise seeds are the surprise ingredients in this familiar old favorite. It's a light but satisfying choice for a main dish, and perfect for a post-holiday supper.

∽

PER SERVING: 301 calories, 27 g protein, 25 g carbohydrates, 10 g total fat, 70 mg cholesterol, 1587 mg sodium

PREPARATION TIME: *15 min.*
COOKING TIME: *45 min.*

1 Tbsp. butter or margarine
1 large onion, thinly sliced,
  separated into rings
1/4 cup pearl barley
1/8 tsp. anise seeds,
  coarsely crushed
1 clove garlic, minced
  or pressed
6 cups chicken broth
3 small carrots, sliced
  1/4-inch thick
1 medium-size orange
2 cups skinned, shredded
  cooked chicken
Chopped parsley

In a 3- to 4-quart pan, melt butter over medium heat. Add onion, barley, and anise seeds. Cook stirring often, until onion is soft (6 to 8 minutes). Stir in garlic; then add broth. Reduce heat, cover, and boil gently until barley is almost tender to bite (about 25 minutes).

Add carrots, cover, and simmer until carrots are just tender (about 10 minutes). Meanwhile, grate enough orange zest to make 1/4 teaspoon; set aside. Cut off and discard remaining peel and white membrane from orange. Lift out orange segments and add to soup along with grated zest and chicken. Cover and summer until chicken is heated through (3 to 5 minutes). Garnish with parsley.

Makes 4 servings

C H I C K E N

Chicken Soup with Matzo Balls

*A popular and traditional opening to a
Passover meal, matzo ball soup is also a good-tasting
dish during any season of the year.*

⌒⌒

PER SERVING: 200 calories, 8 g protein, 18 g carbohydrates, 10 g total fat, 112 mg cholesterol, 1485 mg sodium

PREPARATION TIME: *45 min.*
COOKING TIME: *35 min.*

3 eggs
About 1/3 cup chopped
  parsley
3 Tbsp. water
2 Tbsp. finely chopped onion
3 Tbsp. chicken fat or solid
  vegetable shortening,
  melted and cooled
1 1/4 tsp. salt
*1/8 tsp. **each** ground nutmeg*
  and pepper
3/4 cup matzo meal
6 cups chicken broth
2 medium-size carrots,
  thinly sliced

In a bowl, lightly beat eggs; then stir in 3 tablespoons of the parsley, then the water, onion, chicken fat, salt, nutmeg, and pepper. Add matzo meal and stir until blended. Cover and refrigerate for 30 minutes. With wet hands, shape rounded tablespoonfuls of matzo mixture (it will be slightly sticky) into balls.

In a 2- to 3-quart pan, bring broth to a boil over high heat. Add carrots and matzo balls; reduce heat, cover, and simmer until matzo balls are firm to the touch and a wooden pick inserted in center comes out clean (about 35 minutes). Sprinkle with remaining parsley.

Makes 6 servings

Tortellini & Chicken Soup

CHICKEN

*P*lump tortellini and tender chicken float in a vegetable and rice-filled broth for a simple yet substantial soup. Look for fresh tortellini in the refrigerator case of your supermarket or in a pasta shop.

⌒

PER SERVING: *199 calories, 20 g protein, 21 g carbohydrates, 4 g total fat, 37 mg cholesterol, 1775 mg sodium*

PREPARATION TIME: *15 min.*
COOKING TIME: *15 min.*

4½ qt. chicken broth
1 pkg. (9 oz.) fresh cheese-
   filled spinach tortellini
¾ lb. spinach leaves,
   stemmed
1 lb. boneless, skinless
   chicken breasts, cut into
   ½-inch chunks
½ lb. mushrooms, sliced
1 medium-size red bell
   pepper (about 6 oz.),
   stemmed, seeded, diced
1 cup cooked white or
   brown rice
2 tsp. dry tarragon
   leaves
Grated Parmesan cheese
   (optional)

Rinse, drain and chop spinach leaves. In an 8- to 10-quart pan, bring the chicken broth to a boil over high heat. Add tortellini, and cook until al dente (approximately 4 minutes).

Add spinach, chicken, mushrooms, bell pepper, rice, and tarragon, then return to a boil over high heat. Reduce heat, cover and simmer until chicken in center is no longer pink (about 2 minutes); cut to test. Ladle into bowls and offer with Parmesan cheese, if desired.

Makes 10 to 12 servings

Crunchy
Chicken Salad

*This Sunset Classic lends itself to creative presentation.
Serve on a fresh bed of romaine lettuce or in a shell of crisp
cream puff pastry.*

∽

*PER SERVING (no pastry): 301 calories, 36 g protein, 20 g carbohydrates, 8 g total fat,
95 mg cholesterol, 366 mg sodium*

PREPARATION TIME: *30 min.*
COOKING TIME: *2 min.*

*3 cups cooked chicken
2 tsp. minced fresh cilantro
2 tsp. minced fresh ginger
2 tsp. curry powder
3 Tbsp. seasoned rice
   vinegar (or 3 Tbsp. rice
   vinegar and 3/4 tsp. sugar)
1 cup nonfat yogurt
1 can (8 oz.) sliced water
   chestnuts, drained
Salt to taste
1/2 lb. snow peas
1/2 cup chopped green onions
Romaine lettuce leaves
   or puff pastry
Cilantro leaves*

Mix together chicken, minced cilantro, ginger, curry powder, vinegar, yogurt, and water chestnuts. Add salt to taste. If made ahead, cover and chill until the next day.

Pull stems and strings off snow peas. Drop peas into about 3 quarts rapidly boiling water. Cook, uncovered, just until snow peas are a brighter green (about 2 minutes), then drain. Immerse snow peas in ice water; drain when cool. If made ahead, cover and chill until next day.

Before serving, mix salad with green onions. Arrange snow peas atop crispy romaine lettuce or puff pastry. Add salad; garnish with cilantro leaves.

Makes 4 servings

Chinese Chicken Salad

CHICKEN

Everyday Asian flavors in a refreshing dressing make this dish reminiscent of the popular Chinese chicken salad, but much leaner. Instead of fried noodles as the base, you use lettuce.

⊂⊃

PER SERVING: 208 calories, 23 g protein, 13 g carbohydrates, 8 g total fat, 62 mg cholesterol, 640 mg sodium

PREPARATION TIME: *20 min.*
COOKING TIME: *none*

6 Tbsp. seasoned rice
  vinegar (or 6 Tbsp. rice
  vinegar and 1 Tbsp.
  sugar)
2 tsp. sugar
2 tsp. Oriental sesame oil
1 Tbsp. soy sauce
2¹/2 cups shredded
  cooked chicken
1 cup cherry tomatoes,
  rinsed
8 cups (about 1¹/2 lb.)
  shredded, rinsed, crisped
  iceberg lettuce
¹/2 cup thinly sliced
  green onions
¹/2 cup fresh cilantro leaves
6 to 8 large iceberg lettuce
  leaves, rinsed, crisped

In a large bowl, combine vinegar, sugar, oil, soy sauce, and chicken. Cut cherry tomatoes in half, and add to dressing; stir in shredded lettuce, green onions, and cilantro.

Mound salad equally onto lettuce leaves on individual plates. Add soy sauce to taste.

Makes 4 to 6 servings

Strawberry Chicken Salad

*Strawberries, kiwi fruit, and poultry may sound like
an unusual combination, but in fact, the tart-sweet fruits are
a perfect complement to mild-flavored chicken.*

PER SERVING: *576 calories, 41 g protein, 17 g carbohydrates, 38 g total fat, 125 mg cholesterol, 397 mg sodium*

PREPARATION TIME: *20 min.*
STANDING TIME: *1 hr.*
COOKING TIME: *none*

¹/₂ cup salad oil
*¹/₄ cup strawberry,
  raspberry, or cider
  vinegar*
2 Tbsp. sugar
¹/₂ tsp. **each** *paprika, salt,
  and dry mustard*
*1 green onion, including
  top, finely chopped*
*4 cups bite-size pieces
  cooked chicken*
Butter lettuce leaves
2 cups strawberries, halved
1 or 2 kiwis, peeled, sliced

In a large bowl, stir together salad oil, vinegar, sugar,
paprika, salt, dry mustard and green onion. Stir in
chicken. Cover and let stand for 1 hour.

Line 4 individual plates with lettuce; place about
¹/₂ cup of the strawberries on each plate. With a slotted spoon, lift chicken from dressing; place one-
fourth of the chicken on each plate alongside berries.
Garnish with kiwi slices, then drizzle remaining
dressing over fruit. Serve immediately.

Makes 4 servings

C H I C K E N

Tangy Chicken Salad

Though main-dish salads are associated with warmer days, they can be a welcome touch on a winter menu. This salad pairs chicken with two fruits available all year round.

PER SERVING: *219 calories, 44 g protein, 30 g carbohydrates, 37 g total fat, 125 mg cholesterol, 351 mg sodium*

PREPARATION TIME: *30 min.*
COOKING TIME: *8 min.*
STANDING TIME: *30 min. to 1 hr.*

¹/₃ cup chopped almonds
*¹/₃ cup **each** fresh lemon juice and salad oil*
*2 Tbsp. **each** poppy seeds, honey, and Dijon mustard*
¹/₂ tsp. grated lemon zest
¹/₂ cup moist-pack dried apricots
4 cups bite-size pieces cooked chicken
1 medium-size red apple
¹/₄ cup sliced green onion tops
Salt
Butter lettuce leaves

Spread almonds in a shallow baking pan and toast in a 350° oven until golden brown (about 8 minutes). Set aside.

In a medium-size bowl, stir together lemon juice, oil, poppy seeds, honey, mustard, and lemon zest. Add apricots and stir to coat, then cover and let stand for 30 minutes to 1 hour. Lift out apricots and set aside; stir chicken into dressing. (At this point, you may cover apricots and chicken mixture separately and refrigerate until next day.)

Core and thinly slice apple. Stir apple, onions, and almonds into chicken mixture; season to taste with salt. Line 4 individual plates with lettuce; mound about one-fourth of the chicken salad in the center of each. Garnish each serving with one-fourth of the apricots. Serve immediately.

Makes 4 servings

Minted Chicken & Pineapple Salad

The refreshing flavors of mint and fresh pineapple enliven this chicken salad. The dressing is based on rice vinegar—so mild it needs no oil to balance it.

∞

PER SERVING: 226 calories, 24 g protein, 18 g carbohydrates, 7 g total fat, 73 mg cholesterol, 372 mg sodium

PREPARATION TIME: *30 min.*
CHILLING TIME: *30 min.*

3¹/₂ cups skinned, shredded cooked chicken
³/₄ cup seasoned rice wine vinegar (or ³/₄ cup rice vinegar and 2 Tbsp. sugar)
¹/₄ cup finely chopped fresh mint leaves
1 pineapple (about 3 lb.)
Butter lettuce leaves
Fresh mint sprigs

In a large bowl, combine chicken, vinegar, and chopped mint; mix lightly. Cover and refrigerate for about 30 minutes, stirring occasionally.

Cut off and discard top and bottom of pineapple. Remove rind, cutting deep enough to remove eyes. Cut fruit lengthwise into quarters, remove core, then thinly slice.

Line dinner plates or a large platter with lettuce and arrange pineapple slices on top. With a slotted spoon, lift out the chicken and mound over pineapple; drizzle with vinegar mixture. Garnish with fresh mint sprigs.

Makes 6 servings

Chicken Salad in Cantaloupe Halves

This salad is perfect for brunch on a hot summer's day. For cantaloupe bowls that are steady, slice off a little of the rounded bottom of each melon half.

⌒

PER SERVING: *339 calories, 34 g protein, 34 g carbohydrates, 9 g total fat, 93 mg cholesterol, 229 mg sodium*

PREPARATION TIME: *30 min.*
CHILLING TIME: *up to 4 hr.*

1 small (about 6 oz.)
  yellow bell pepper
1 medium-size (about 1 lb.)
  firm-ripe papaya
3 cups shredded cooked
  chicken
1/4 cup minced fresh
  cilantro leaves
2 Tbsp. drained canned
  capers
2 tsp. grated lime peel
1/4 cup **each** lime juice
  and orange juice
2 small cantaloupes
  (each about 2 1/4 lb.),
  cut into halves, seeded
Lime wedges (optional)
Salt and pepper

Stem and seed bell pepper; finely dice pepper. Cut papaya into halves and discard seed; peel fruit and cut into about 3/8-inch cubes.

Combine bell pepper, papaya, chicken, cilantro, and capers. (If making ahead, cover and chill up to 4 hours.) Stir together lime peel, lime juice, and orange juice. Pour citrus juices over chicken mixture; stir to mix.

Spoon chicken equally into melon halves; garnish with lime. Add salt and pepper to taste.

Makes 4 servings

BEST OF EAST & WEST

Hot & Sweet Chicken

*A tangy, citrus-based sauce does double duty in this dish.
You use part of it to coat a cut-up chicken during baking, then mix the rest
with the pan juices to spoon over the cooked meat and hot, fluffy rice.*

⌒

PER SERVING: *741 calories, 49 g protein, 81 g carbohydrates, 23 g total fat, 143 mg cholesterol, 364 mg sodium*

PREPARATION TIME: *10 min.*
COOKING TIME: *55 min.*

1 Tbsp. grated orange peel
1 cup orange juice
3 Tbsp. lemon juice
2 Tbsp. Worcestershire
  sauce
1 Tbsp. Dijon mustard
1/2 tsp. liquid hot pepper
  seasoning
1/2 cup red currant jelly
1 chicken (3 to 3 1/2 lb.),
  cut up
3 cups hot cooked rice
1 Tbsp. cornstarch mixed
  with 2 Tbsp. water

In a pan, combine first 7 ingredients. Stir over medium heat until jelly melts.

Rinse chicken and pat dry; then arrange, except breast pieces, skin side up in a shallow roasting pan. Brush with some of the orange sauce. Bake, uncovered, in a 400° oven for 20 minutes, basting with sauce after 10 minutes. Add breast pieces. Continue to bake, basting often, until meat near thighbone is no longer pink (about 25 more minutes); cut to test.

Arrange chicken and rice on a platter; keep warm. Discard fat from pan juices, then add remaining orange sauce. Add cornstarch mixture and bring to a boil over high heat, stirring. Serve sauce with meal.

Makes 4 servings

Sesame Chicken & Vegetables

C H I C K E N

A bed of stir-fried red cabbage and emerald snow peas provides a crisp, colorful contrast to these grilled chicken breasts sprinkled with sesame seeds.

༺༻

PER SERVING: 400 calories, 40 g protein, 40 g carbohydrates, 8 g total fat, 86 mg cholesterol, 454 mg sodium

PREPARATION TIME: *20 min.*
COOKING TIME: *15 min.*

4 chicken breast halves
  (about 2 lb. total),
  skinned, boned
1 tsp. sesame seeds
Vegetable oil cooking spray
*4 tsp. **each** rice vinegar*
  and soy sauce
1½ tsp. Oriental sesame oil
1 Tbsp. grated fresh ginger
2 cloves garlic, minced
  or pressed
½ tsp. sugar
1 Tbsp. vegetable oil
8 oz. mushrooms, sliced
4 cups thinly sliced
  red cabbage
4 oz. snow peas, ends
  and strings removed
2 cups hot cooked rice

Rinse chicken, pat dry, and sprinkle with sesame seeds. Spray a ridged cooktop grill pan with cooking spray. Place over medium heat and preheat until a drop of water dances on the surface. Then place chicken on grill and cook, turning once, until well browned on outside and no longer pink in thickest part (12 to 15 minutes); cut to test.

Meanwhile, in a small bowl, stir together vinegar, soy sauce, sesame oil, ginger, garlic, and sugar; set aside. Then heat vegetable oil in a large nonstick frying pan over medium-high heat. Add mushrooms and cook, stirring often, for about 3 minutes. Add cabbage and cook, stirring often, until it begins to soften (about 2 minutes). Add snow peas and cook, stirring, just until they turn bright green (1 to 2 minutes). Add vinegar mixture; stir for 1 more minute.

Cut each chicken piece diagonally across the grain into ½-inch-wide strips. Arrange chicken over vegetables on warm dinner plates; serve with rice.

Makes 4 servings

Chicken Kung Pao Style

*This version of Szechwan's kung pao is a bit milder
than its fiery traditional counterpart. This is a wok or skillet
specialty suited for casual and elegant occasions alike.*

∾

PER SERVING: *472 calories, 48 g protein, 24 g carbohydrates, 18 g total fat, 114 mg cholesterol, 1509 mg sodium*

PREPARATION TIME: *15 min.*
STANDING TIME: *1 hr.*
COOKING TIME: *15 min.*

*2 whole chicken breasts
(about 1 lb. each),
skinned, boned, split*
2 Tbsp. cornstarch
*3 tbsp. **each** soy sauce,
water, and dry sherry*
2 Tbsp. hoisin sauce
1 tsp. Oriental sesame oil
3 Tbsp. salad oil
6 small dried hot red chiles
2 cloves garlic, minced
*3/4 cup sliced green onions
(including tops)*
*1 can (8 oz.) water chest-
nuts, drained, sliced*

Rinse chicken and pat dry; cut into 3/4-inch chunks.
In a bowl, stir together cornstarch, soy sauce, water,
and sherry. Add chicken and mix well; then cover
and let stand for 1 hour.

Lift chicken from marinade and drain briefly,
reserving marinade; set aside. Stir hoisin sauce and
sesame oil into marinade; set aside.

Place a wok or large frying pan over high heat.
When pan is hot, add salad oil. When oil begins to
heat, add chicken and cook, stirring, until lightly
browned (about 3 minutes). Lift out and set aside.

Add chiles to pan and cook, stirring, until black.
Add garlic and all but 1 tablespoon of the onions;
cook, stirring, for 15 seconds. Return chicken to pan
with water chestnuts and marinade; cook, stirring,
until sauce boils and thickens. Spoon chicken mixture into a serving dish and sprinkle with the
reserved onions.

Makes 3 to 4 servings

C H I C K E N

Chicken & Olive Sauté

Only the dark pieces of chicken are used in this succulent Spanish-style dish. Fresh or frozen chard is served with it to complement the sauce.

PER SERVING: *474 calories, 32 g protein, 8 g carbohydrates, 35g total fat, 138 mg cholesterol, 897 mg sodium*

PREPARATION TIME: *10 min.*
COOKING TIME: *1 hr.*

¼ cup olive oil
1 medium-size onion, chopped
2 cloves garlic
*6 **each** chicken drumsticks and thighs, separated*
Salt
½ cup canned tomato sauce
¼ cup water
1 can (7½ oz.) pitted green or ripe black olives, drained
1 jar (2¼ oz.) pimento-stuffed Spanish-style olives, drained
4 cups packed chopped Swiss chard or 2 pkg. (12 oz. each) frozen Swiss chard, thawed

Heat oil in a large frying pan over medium heat. Add onion and garlic and cook, stirring, until onion is soft; remove from pan with a slotted spoon and set aside. Sprinkle chicken with salt. Raise heat to medium high and brown chicken lightly on all sides. Return onion and garlic to pan, then add tomato sauce, water, and both kinds of olives. Reduce heat to low, cover pan, and simmer gently until chicken is quite tender when pierced (40 minutes).

About 10 minutes before chicken is done, stir in fresh chard, cover and continue to cook. (If using frozen chard, add 5 minutes before chicken is done.)

Transfer chicken pieces to a wide serving dish. With a slotted spoon, lift out chard and spoon alongside chicken. Remove garlic from sauce, if desired. Over high heat, boil sauce rapidly to reduce slightly, then pour over chicken and chard.

Makes 6 servings

Roasted Chicken Teriyaki

*Anise-teriyaki sauce seasons a main course
of oven-cooked chicken—delicious served with
spaghetti squash and roasted onions.*

∽

PER SERVING: *768 calories, 62 g protein, 7 g carbohydrates, 53 g total fat, 246 mg cholesterol, 1002 mg sodium*

PREPARATION TIME: *20 min.*
COOKING TIME: *1 1/4 hr.*

1 Tbsp. salad oil
1 tsp. anise seed
3 Tbsp. **each** orange juice
  and soy sauce
1 Tbsp. **each** sugar and dry
  sherry or any dry wine
1 clove garlic, minced
  or pressed
1 Tbsp. minced fresh ginger
1 broiler-fryer chicken
  (4 to 4 1/2 lb.)
1 spaghetti squash, baked,
  peeled, seeded
2 large yellow onions,
  halved, roasted

In a 1- to 1 1/2-quart pan on medium heat, stir oil with anise seed until hot. Add orange juice, soy sauce, sugar, sherry, garlic, and ginger; set teriyaki sauce aside.

Rinse chicken and pat dry; reserve giblets for other uses. Put chicken, breast up, on a rack in a 9- by 13-inch pan; coat generously with teriyaki sauce. Pour remaining sauce into cavity of bird. Roast, uncovered, in a 375° oven. After chicken has roasted 30 minutes, add 1/4 cup water to the pan. Cook until chicken is no longer pink at thighbone, about 1 1/4 hours; cut to test.

Drain juices from chicken cavity into pan, then put bird on a platter and keep warm. Stir to free browned bits in pan. Measure juices; if more than 2/3 cup, place pan on high heat and boil until reduced to about 2/3 cup. Keep warm and use to flavor baked spaghetti squash and roasted onions to accompany meal.

Makes 4 servings

Chicken Jambalaya

This hearty Cajun casserole can warm up your party and your palate. Seasoned with plenty of red pepper, jambalaya is definitely not for timid tastes!

∽

PER SERVING: 475 calories, 42 g protein, 58 g carbohydrates, 8 g total fat, 85 mg cholesterol, 1566 mg sodium

PREPARATION TIME: *45 min.*
COOKING TIME: *45 min.*

1 Tbsp. salad oil
1/2 lb. diced Canadian bacon
1 1/2 lb. skinned, boned
    chicken breasts, cut into
    bite-size chunks
1 large onion, chopped
3 cloves garlic, pressed
2 large green bell peppers,
    seeded, chopped
1 cup chopped celery
6 large tomatoes, chopped
1 large can (15 oz.)
    tomato sauce
2 bay leaves, crumbled
1 tsp. dry thyme leaves
2 tsp. ground white pepper
1 tsp. cayenne pepper
1/2 cup chopped parsley
1 1/2 cups long-grain
    white rice
3 cups chicken broth

Heat oil in a 12- to 14-inch frying pan over medium heat. Add Canadian bacon and chicken; cook, stirring often, until browned on all sides (about 6 minutes). Transfer chicken to a 4- to 5-quart casserole.

Add onion, garlic, bell peppers, and celery to pan. Cook, stirring occasionally, until onion is soft (about 10 minutes). Add tomatoes, tomato sauce, bay leaves, thyme, white pepper, cayenne pepper, and parsley; cook, stirring occasionally, until sauce boils. Boil gently, uncovered, for 5 minutes.

Pour sauce over chicken; stir in rice and broth. Cover and bake in a 375° oven until rice is tender to bite (about 45 minutes).

Makes 6 servings

Golden Chicken Cutlets

Serve these crisp, herb-seasoned chicken cutlets hot or cold, for a picnic or summer buffet, or any casual occasion.

PER SERVING: *371 calories, 39 g protein, 11 g carbohydrates, 17 g total fat, 145 mg cholesterol, 527 mg sodium*

PREPARATION TIME: *25 min.*
COOKING TIME: *15 min.*

*3 whole chicken breasts
   (about 1 lb. each),
   skinned, boned, split*
¼ cup all-purpose flour
½ tsp. salt
*⅛ tsp. **each** white pepper,
   ground nutmeg, and
   marjoram leaves*
1 egg
1 Tbsp. water
*½ cup fine dry bread
   crumbs*
*⅓ cup grated
   Parmesan cheese*
¼ cup butter or margarine
2 Tbsp. olive oil or salad oil
½ cup dry white wine
Lemon wedges

Rinse chicken and pat dry. Place pieces, one at a time, skinned side down, between 2 sheets of plastic wrap, and pound with a flat-surfaced mallet until about ¼ inch thick.

In a dish, mix flour, salt, pepper, nutmeg, and marjoram. Beat egg and water in a second dish; mix bread crumbs and cheese in a third. Coat chicken with flour mixture, then egg, then crumb mixture.

Melt butter in oil in a large frying pan over medium-high heat. Add half the chicken breasts; cook, turning after 2 to 3 minutes, until no longer pink when slashed (4 to 6 minutes total). Transfer to a platter and keep warm. Repeat with the remaining chicken.

Add wine to pan; boil over high heat until slightly reduced, stirring to scrape browned bits free. Pour over the chicken. Offer lemon wedges to squeeze over meat.

Makes 6 servings

Chicken Breasts Véronique

As "Véronique" suggests,
*this handsome presentation of chicken breasts
features green grapes.*

PER SERVING: *280 calories, 35 g protein, 8 g carbohydrates, 10 g total fat, 114 mg cholesterol, 134 mg sodium*

PREPARATION TIME: *10 min.*
COOKING TIME: *30 min.*

*4 whole chicken breasts
(about 1 lb. each),
skinned, boned, split
2 Tbsp. butter or margarine
1 1/2 Tbsp. orange
marmalade
1/2 tsp. dry tarragon
1/2 cup dry white wine
1/2 cup whipping cream
Salt
1 1/2 cups seedless
green grapes*

Rinse chicken and pat dry. Melt butter in a large frying pan over medium heat. Add chicken, a portion at a time, without crowding; cook, turning once, until lightly browned on both sides.

Stir in marmalade, tarragon, and wine. Bring to a boil over high heat; then reduce heat, cover, and simmer, turning once, until meat is no longer pink when slashed in thickest part (about 15 minutes). Transfer chicken to a serving dish; keep warm. Add cream to pan juices; boil, stirring, until slightly reduced. Season to taste with salt, then mix in grapes and return to a boil. Pour over chicken.

Makes 8 servings

Spinach-stuffed
Chicken Breasts

C H I C K E N

*When carefully slit in the thickest part,
chicken breasts make neat "pockets" for a
spinach stuffing.*

✆

PER SERVING: *410 calories, 51 g protein, 7 g carbohydrates, 18 g total fat, 160 mg cholesterol, 492 mg sodium*

PREPARATION TIME: *35 min.*
COOKING TIME: *30 min.*

*8 slices bacon
1 large onion, finely chopped
1 package (10 oz.) frozen
   chopped spinach, thawed,
   squeezed dry
1 egg, lightly beaten
1/2 cup seasoned croutons,
   coarsely crushed
1/2 tsp. garlic salt
4 whole chicken breasts
   (about 1 lb. each),
   skinned, boned, split
3 Tbsp. salad oil*

In a large frying pan, cook bacon over medium heat until crisp; then lift out, drain, crumble, and set aside. Discard all but 2 tablespoons of the drippings.

Add onion to pan and cook, stirring, until soft; remove pan from heat, then stir in spinach, egg, croutons, garlic salt, and bacon.

Rinse chicken and pat dry. With a sharp knife, cut a deep pocket in the thick side of each breast half, to within about 1 inch of short ends and other long side. Stuff each breast half with one-eighth of the spinach mixture, and fasten each one closed with wooden picks.

Wipe frying pan clean. Add oil and heat over medium heat. Add half the chicken; cook, turning after 6 to 7 minutes, until meat is no longer pink when slashed (12 to 15 minutes *total*). Repeat until all the chicken is cooked.

Makes 6 servings

Garlic Chicken & Potatoes

*Don't let the amount of garlic keep you from trying this
hearty combination of chicken and potatoes; with long, gentle simmering,
the pungent cloves take on a surprisingly mild, sweet flavor.*

☜☞

PER SERVING: *489 calories, 30 g protein, 28 g carbohydrates, 28 g total fat, 121 mg cholesterol, 128 mg sodium*

PREPARATION TIME: *15 min.*
COOKING TIME: *35 to 40 min.*

*4 whole chicken legs
   (1½ to 2 lb. total)*
3 Tbsp. olive oil or salad oil
*8 small red thin-skinned
   potatoes (each 1½ to
   2 inches in diameter),
   scrubbed*
*1½ tsp. minced fresh
   rosemary or 1 tsp. dry
   rosemary*
¼ cup water
*24 large cloves garlic, peeled
   and slightly crushed*
Salt and pepper
Rosemary sprigs (optional)

Rinse chicken and pat dry. Heat oil in a large frying pan over medium-high heat. Add chicken and potatoes; cook, turning potatoes occasionally and chicken once, until chicken pieces are browned on both sides (10 to 12 minutes).

Reduce heat to low and add minced rosemary and water to pan. Cover and cook for 15 minutes. Turn chicken again and add garlic. Cover and continue to cook, turning potatoes and garlic occasionally, until potatoes are tender throughout when pierced and meat near thighbone is no longer pink (about 10 more minutes); cut to test. Transfer chicken, potatoes, and garlic to a warm platter.

Stir pan drippings, scraping browned bits free; pour over chicken and vegetables. Season to taste with salt and pepper. Garnish with rosemary sprigs, if desired.

Makes 4 servings

HOT OFF THE GRILL

C H I C K E N

Chicken for a Hungry Dozen

*This chicken is topped with the thick, sweet-sour
red barbecue sauce that's popular with almost everybody.
The sauce keeps for two weeks in the refrigerator.*

PER SERVING: *469 calories, 45 g protein, 15 g carbohydrates, 24 g total fat, 143 mg cholesterol, 508 mg sodium*

PREPARATION TIME: *55 min.*
GRILLING TIME: *40 to 50 min.*

2 Tbsp. salad oil
1 medium-size onion,
 chopped
3 cans (8 oz. each)
 tomato sauce
½ cup red wine vinegar
½ cup firmly packed
 brown sugar
2 Tbsp. Worcestershire
 sauce
1 tsp. cracked pepper
3 frying chickens (3 to
 3½ lb. each), quartered

Heat salad oil in a 3-quart pan over medium heat.
Add onion; cook, stirring often, until soft (about 10
minutes). Stir in tomato sauce, vinegar, brown sugar,
Worchestershire sauce, and pepper. Bring to a boil;
then reduce heat and simmer, uncovered, until thick-
ened (about 45 minutes). Stir occasionally to prevent
sticking. Set aside or, if made ahead, let cool, then
cover and refrigerate.

Rinse chicken, pat dry, and place on a lightly
greased grill 4 to 6 inches above a solid bed of medium coals. Cook, turning occasionally, for 20 minutes;
then brush generously with barbecue sauce. Continue
to cook, turning and basting several times, until meat
near thighbone is no longer pink (20 to 30 more minutes); cut to test. Heat any remaining sauce and offer
at the table to spoon over individual servings.

Makes 12 servings

Chili-glazed Chicken
with Peas

CHICKEN

Try serving iced tea and margaritas with this lime- and chili-charged chicken. A buttery baste helps keep the pieces moist—and makes them especially flavorful, too.

⊂⊃

PER SERVING: *556 calories, 51 g protein, 18 g carbohydrates, 30 g total fat, 164 mg cholesterol, 226 mg sodium*

PREPARATION TIME: *5 min.*
GRILLING TIME: *40 min.*

1 chicken (3 to 3½ lb.),
  cut in eighths
⅓ cup butter or
  margarine, melted
2 cloves garlic, minced
  or pressed
1 tsp. chili powder
*¼ tsp. **each** ground cumin*
  and grated lime peel
2 Tbsp. lime juice
2 lb. peas in the pod
2 Tbsp. water

Rinse chicken and pat dry. In a small pan, stir together butter, garlic, chili powder, cumin, lime peel, and lime juice. Brush generously over chicken.

Arrange chicken, except breast pieces, skin side up on a lightly greased grill 4 to 6 inches above a solid bed of medium coals. Cook for 15 minutes, turning and basting frequently with butter mixture. Place breast pieces on grill. Continue to cook, turning and basting often, until meat near thighbone is no longer pink (about 25 more minutes); cut to test.

Meanwhile, rinse the peas; then place in a cast-iron frying pan or Dutch oven and add water. Cover with lid or foil; place on grill next to chicken during last 15 minutes of cooking, stirring peas every 5 minutes. Let guests shell their own peas to eat alongside the chicken.

Makes 4 servings

Herb-mustard Chicken

*A basic marinade gains a zesty
new dimension from spicy brown mustard. If you like
mustard, experiment with other varieties.*

PER SERVING: *570 calories, 45 g protein, 2 g carbohydrates, 41 g total fat, 143 mg cholesterol, 214 mg sodium*

PREPARATION TIME: *10 min.*
MARINATING TIME: *4 hr.*
GRILLING TIME: *40 min.*

*1 frying chicken,
   (3 to 3½ lb.), cut
   in eighths
½ cup dry white wine
⅔ cup salad oil
6 Tbsp. white wine vinegar
2 Tbsp. finely chopped onion
1 tsp. Italian herb seasoning
   or thyme leaves
2 cloves garlic, minced
   or pressed
½ tsp. pepper
¼ cup spicy brown mustard*

Rinse chicken and pat dry. In a large bowl, stir together wine, oil, vinegar, onion, herb seasoning, garlic, pepper, and mustard. Reserve ¼ cup of marinade. Add chicken to remaining marinade and turn to coat. Cover and refrigerate for at least 4 hours or until next day, turning occasionally.

Lift chicken from marinade and drain briefly. Place chicken, except breast pieces, skin side up on a lightly greased grill 4 to 6 inches above a solid bed of medium coals. Cook, turning and basting frequently with reserved marinade for 15 minutes. Place breast pieces on grill and continue to cook, turning and basting often, until meat near bone is no longer pink (about 25 more minutes); cut to test.

Makes about 4 servings

CHICKEN

Rosemary Chicken Quarters

For best flavor,
start this chicken marinating at least
3 hours before you barbecue.

PER SERVING: 511 calories, 44 g protein, .68 g carbohydrates, 36 g total fat, 143 mg cholesterol, 134 mg sodium

PREPARATION TIME: *10 min.*
MARINATING TIME: *3 hr.*
GRILLING TIME: *40-50 min.*

1 frying chicken
(3 to 3½ lb.), quartered
½ cup olive oil or salad oil
2 tsp. dry rosemary
1 tsp. finely chopped parsley
2 cloves garlic, minced
or pressed
2 Tbsp. lemon juice
⅛ tsp. pepper

Rinse chicken and pat dry. In a large bowl, combine oil, rosemary, parsley, garlic, lemon juice, and pepper. Reserve 2 tablespoons of marinade. Turn chicken in remaining marinade to coat. Cover and refrigerate for at least 3 hours or until next day, turning occasionally.

Lift chicken from marinade and drain briefly. Place chicken, skin side up, on a lightly greased grill 4 to 6 inches above a solid bed of medium coals. Cook (40 to 50 minutes), turning and basting frequently with reserved marinade until meat near thighbone is no longer pink; cut to test.

Spanish-Style
Chicken

*This barbecue adaptation of Spain's famous
"arroz con pollo" (rice with chicken) is well complemented
by tiny marinated artichokes and cherry tomatoes.*

⬡

PER SERVING: 897 calories, 55 g protein, 58 g carbohydrates, 48 g total fat, 202 mg cholesterol, 598 mg sodium

PREPARATION TIME: *35 min.*
GRILLING TIME: *40 to 50 min.*

*1 frying chicken
(3 to 3½ lb.), quartered
½ cup (¼ lb.) butter or
margarine, melted
1 clove garlic, minced
or pressed
¾ tsp. savory
½ tsp. paprika
¼ tsp. **each** ground cinnamon and dry tarragon*

*CHORIZO RICE:
2 chorizo sausages (2½
to 3 oz. each), cut
into ½-inch slices
2 medium-size onions,
finely chopped
3 cups cooked rice
1 cup frozen peas, thawed
1 tomato*

Rinse chicken and pat dry. In a bowl, combine butter, garlic, savory, paprika, cinnamon, and tarragon.
Turn chicken in butter mixture to coat, then lift out
and drain briefly; reserve butter mixture. Place chick-
en, skin side up, on a lightly greased grill 4 to 6 inches above a solid bed of medium coals. Cook, turning
and basting frequently with butter mixture, until
meat near thighbone is no longer pink (40 to 50
minutes); cut to test.

Meanwhile prepare chorizo rice: Cook chorizo in
a wide frying pan over medium heat until browned
on all sides. Pour off all but 2 tablespoons of fat. Add
onions; cook, stirring occasionally, until soft. Stir in
rice, peas and tomato. Cover and cook over low heat
until hot throughout (about 10 minutes); then blend
in 1 to 2 tablespoons of reserved butter mixture.

Makes 4 servings

Chicken with Brandy Baste

*Chicken and fruit are always good together.
Here, apricots and dark sweet cherries join juicy chicken
quarters brushed with a buttery brandy baste.*

∽

PER SERVING: *525 calories, 45 g protein, 11 g carbohydrates, 31 g total fat, 166 mg cholesterol, 224 mg sodium*

PREPARATION TIME: *20 min.*
GRILLING TIME: *40 to 50 min.*

*2 frying chickens
(3 to 3¹/₂ lb. each),
quartered*
Pepper
*¹/₂ cup (¹/₄ lb.) butter or
margarine, melted*
*¹/₄ cup **each** firmly packed
brown sugar, lemon
juice, and brandy*
*6 fresh apricots, halved,
pitted (or 12 canned
apricot halves, drained)*
*1 cup pitted fresh dark sweet
cherries (or canned pitted
dark sweet cherries,
drained)*

Rinse chicken and pat dry. Sprinkle with pepper.
In a bowl, combine butter, sugar, lemon juice, and
brandy. Reserve ¹/₄ cup of butter mixture. Brush
chicken with remaining butter mixture to coat.

Place chicken, skin side up, on a lightly greased
grill 4 to 6 inches above a solid bed of medium coals.
Cover barbecue and adjust dampers (or cover with a
tent of heavy-duty foil). Cook, turning and basting
occasionally with reserved butter mixture, until the
meat near the thighbone is no longer pink (40 to 50
minutes); cut to test.

Meanwhile, arrange apricots (cut side up) and
cherries in 2 separate shallow metal baking pans.
Brush fruit with reserved butter mixture, then heat
on grill beside chicken for last 5 to 10 minutes of
cooking.

To serve, place chicken on a platter and surround
with apricots; pour cherries over top.

Makes 8 servings

C H I C K E N

Savory Herb Chicken

*Sherry, garlic, and four kinds of herbs
punctuate the marinade for these simple
grilled chicken quarters.*

∽

PER SERVING: *465 calories, 45 g protein, 4 g carbohydrates, 29 g total fat, 143 mg cholesterol, 177 mg sodium*

PREPARATION TIME: *15 min.*
MARINATING TIME: *1 hr.*
GRILLING TIME: *40 to 50 min.*

*2 frying chickens
(3 to 3½ lb. each),
quartered
1 cup dry sherry
½ cup salad oil
1 large onion, finely chopped
1 Tbsp. Worcestershire sauce
1 tsp. **each** garlic powder,
thyme leaves, oregano
leaves, marjoram leaves,
dry rosemary, soy sauce,
and lemon juice*

Rinse chicken and pat dry. In a large bowl, combine sherry, oil, onion, Worcestershire sauce, garlic powder, thyme, oregano, marjoram, rosemary, soy sauce, and lemon juice. Reserve ½ cup of marinade. Turn chicken in remaining marinade to coat; then cover and refrigerate for at least 1 hour or until next day, turning occasionally.

Lift chicken from marinade and drain briefly. Place chicken, skin side up, on a lightly greased grill 4 to 6 inches above a solid bed of medium coals. Cook, turning frequently, until meat near thighbone is no longer pink (40 to 50 minutes); cut to test.

Makes 8 servings

Chicken Wings
with Grilled Potatoes

If you're looking for a good picnic entrée, consider these grilled marinated chicken wings and garlicky potato slices. For easy turning, arrange the wings in a hinged barbecue basket before placing them on the grill.

◠◠

PER SERVING: *839 calories, 52 g protein, 47 g carbohydrates, 49 g total fat, 175 mg cholesterol, 1306 mg sodium*

PREPARATION TIME: *15 min.*
MARINATING TIME: *2 hr.*
GRILLING TIME: *30 min.*

*20 chicken wings
(about 4 lb.)*
¹/₂ cup soy sauce
*1 clove garlic, minced
or pressed*
1 tsp. ground ginger
*2 Tbsp. **each** firmly packed
brown sugar, lemon juice,
and salad oil*
*1 Tbsp. instant
minced onion*
¹/₄ tsp. pepper
4 large russet potatoes
Melted butter or margarine
Garlic salt

Rinse chicken wings and pat dry. Bend wings open. In a large bowl, stir together soy sauce, garlic, ginger, sugar, lemon juice, oil, onion, and pepper. Stir in wings; cover and refrigerate for 2 hours, stirring several times.

Scrub potatoes, but do not peel. Cut lengthwise into ¹/₄-inch slices; brush generously with butter and sprinkle with garlic salt.

Lift chicken from marinade and drain briefly; discard marinade. Place chicken and potato slices on a lightly greased grill 4 to 6 inches above a solid bed of medium coals. Cook, turning chicken and potatoes occasionally, until potatoes are soft when pierced and meat near bone is no longer pink (about 30 minutes); cut to test.

Makes about 4 servings

Chicken-on-a-stick
with Couscous

*Compose a balanced meal with little effort
by offering chicken kebabs, fluffy couscous,
and a calcium-rich yogurt sauce.*

∽

PER SERVING: *605 calories, 50 g protein, 66 g carbohydrates, 14 g total fat, 91 mg cholesterol, 202 mg sodium*

PREPARATION TIME: *30 min.*
MARINATING TIME: *30 min.*
GRILLING TIME: *10 min.*

*1¹/₂ cups plain lowfat yogurt
2 Tbsp. minced cilantro
1 tsp. cumin seeds
7 cloves garlic, minced
  or pressed
¹/₃ cup **each** lemon juice
  and olive oil
¹/₄ cup dry white wine
2 bay leaves, crumbled
2 whole chicken breasts
  (about 1 lb. each),
  skinned, boned, split,
  cut into ³/₄-inch chunks
2¹/₂ cups low-sodium
  chicken broth
10 oz. (about 1³/₄ cups)
  couscous
¹/₂ cup sliced green onions
  (including tops)*

Soak 8 bamboo skewers in hot water to cover for
at least 30 minutes Meanwhile, stir together yogurt,
cilantro, cumin seeds, and 1 minced clove garlic;
cover and refrigerate for at least 15 minutes.

In a medium-size bowl, mix lemon juice, oil,
wine, remaining garlic, and bay leaves. Reserve ¹/₄
cup of marinade. Add chicken to remaining marinade, turning to coat. Cover and refrigerate for 30
minutes, or up to 4 hours.

In a 2- to-3-quart pan, bring chicken broth to a
boil over high heat. Stir in couscous. Cover, remove
from heat, and let stand.

Thread chicken on skewers. Place on a lightly
greased grill 4 to 6 inches above medium-hot coals.
Cook, basting with reserved marinade, turning as
needed, until meat in center is no longer pink (about
10 minutes); cut to test.

Stir onions into couscous and fluff. Spoon onto a
platter and top with skewers. Offer yogurt sauce.

Makes 4 servings (2 skewers each)

Garlic-basted Chicken

M*any people insist that garlic is "good for what ails you."*
We know it's good for flavoring chicken, especially when combined
with the subtle hop overtones from beer.

PER SERVING: *342 calories, 29 g protein, 1 g carbohydrates, 23 g total fat, 125 mg cholesterol, 180 mg sodium*

PREPARATION TIME: *15 min.*
GRILLING TIME: *20 to 45 min.,*
  depending on chicken parts

6 whole chicken legs, with
  thighs attached (about
  3 lb. total); or 3 whole
  chicken breasts (about
  1 lb. each), split
1/2 cup (1/4 lb.) butter
  or margarine
4 cloves garlic, minced
  or pressed
1/4 cup finely chopped onion
1 cup beer
1 Tbsp. finely
  chopped parsley
1/2 tsp. coarsely ground
  pepper

Rinse chicken and pat dry. Melt butter in a small pan over medium heat; add garlic and onion and cook, stirring occasionally, until onion is soft. Add beer and bring to a boil, stirring. Remove from heat. Stir in parsley and pepper; pour into a large bowl. Turn chicken in butter mixture to coat, then remove chitcken from the bowl; reserve butter mixture.

Place chicken, skin side up, on a lightly greased grill 4 to 6 inches above a solid bed of medium coals. Cook, turning and basting frequently with butter mixture, until meat near bone is no longer pink (35 to 45 minutes for legs, 20 to 25 minutes for breasts); cut to test.

Makes 6 servings

Tandoori Chicken

A *paste of fresh ginger, garlic, and spices tucked
under the skin of whole chicken legs gives the meat a pleasant bite.
Temper the heat with spoonfuls of cold yogurt.*

PER SERVING: *297 calories, 33 g protein, 1 g carbohydrates, 17 g total fat, 116 mg cholesterol, 111 mg sodium*

PREPARATION TIME: *20 min.*
GRILLING TIME: *35 to 45 min.*

*4 whole chicken legs,
  thighs attached
  (2 to 2½ lb. total)
1 tsp. **each** grated fresh
  ginger and ground allspice
¼ to ½ tsp. crushed
  red pepper
2 cloves garlic, minced
  or pressed
1 Tbsp. lemon juice
Plain yogurt*

Rinse chicken and pat dry. In a bowl, mash together ginger, allspice, red pepper, garlic, and lemon juice to make a paste. Then lift skin of each chicken leg; spread 1 teaspoon paste over flesh of thigh and top of drumstick. Brush any remaining paste evenly over the skin.

Place chicken, skin side up, on a lightly greased grill 4 to 6 inches above a solid bed of medium coals. Cook, turning frequently, until meat near thighbone is no longer pink (35 to 45 minutes); cut to test. Offer cold yogurt to spoon over chicken.

Makes 4 servings

Chicken &
Fruit Kebabs

Juicy chunks of pineapple and papaya pair beautifully with sherry and soy-flavored chicken. You thread the fruit on skewers and start the chicken marinating in advance; actual cooking time is less than 15 minutes.

∽

PER SERVING: *413 calories, 53 g protein, 25 g carbohydrates, 10 g total fat, 129 mg cholesterol, 534 mg sodium*

PREPARATION TIME: *30 min.*
MARINATING TIME: *1 hr.*
COOKING TIME: *10 to 15 min.*

3 whole chicken breasts (about 1½ lb. each), skinned, boned, split
⅓ cup dry sherry
*3 Tbsp. **each** soy sauce and sesame oil*
1½ tsp. finely chopped fresh ginger
1 large papaya, peeled, seeded, cut into 1½-inch chunks
1 pineapple (3 to 3½ lb.), peeled, cored, cut into 1½-inch chunks
2 Tbsp. sesame seeds, toasted until golden

Rinse chicken and pat dry. Cut each breast half into 6 or 7 equal-size chunks. Stir together sherry, soy sauce, sesame oil, and ginger; pour ¼ of marinade into a bowl; reserve the remainder. Add chicken to marinade in bowl and mix gently to coat. Cover and let stand for 1 hour, or refrigerate for up to 8 hours.

Drain marinated chicken briefly; thread chicken on six 12-inch-long skewers. Alternating papaya and pineapple, thread fruit on six more skewers.

Place chicken on grill 4 to 6 inches above a solid bed of low-glowing coals. Cook, turning occasionally, until meat is no longer pink when slashed (10 to 12 minutes); cut to test.

Meanwhile, brush fruit with a little of the reserved marinade. Place on grill next to chicken and cook, turning occasionally, just until heated through and lightly browned (about 3 minutes).

To serve, sprinkle chicken and fruit with sesame seeds.

Makes about 6 servings

Index